UNCHAINABLE SPIRIT

Poems in Memory of the Wobbly Hobo Monk

Michael Adams
1949 - 2013

Edited by RD Armstrong

©2014 by RD Armstrong

All photographs used by permission of Claire Mearns

All poems used by permission of the authors

All Rights Reserved

No part of this book may be used without the express written permission of the editor.

ISBN 978-1-929878-71-0

First edition

PO Box 5301
San Pedro, CA 90733
www.lummoxpress.com

Printed in the United States of America

Special thanks to: Jared Smith, Phil Woods, Jerry Smaldone, Deborah Kelly, Padma Thornlyre, Judyth Hill, Linn G. Baker, Roseanna Frechette, John Macker, Rosemerry Wahtola Trommer, Art Goodtimes, Claire Mearns, Stewart Warren, G. Murray Thomas, Lawrence Gladeview, Jim Bernath, James Taylor III and Mike Adams, who made this possible by his presence in our lives.

Tough Old Buzzard

TABLE OF CONTENTS

- 5   Say Goodbye
- 7   AveAtqueVale
- 8   Poet Goes
- 9   Gratitude
- 10 Melting Snow
- 11 Mu
- 13 For Michael Adams
- 14 It's All About Stone
- 15 I Lent Steel Valley
- 16 Last Words for a Shaman
- 17 October Twilight
- 18 Strawbale
- 20 The Last Lonesome Stars of Colorado
- 22 Nothing Much Has Changed
- 22 Everything is in Front of Us
- 24 Mike 3
- 26 Practicing Tai Chi in Elks Park
- 26 The Day After He Died
- 28 On The Death of Mike Adams
- 29 Lone Wolf
- 30 Elegy for Michael Adams
- 36 Too Soon
- 37 For All of Us

- 39 About Michael Adams

Say Goodbye by Michael Adams

say goodbye to her, the Alexandria that is leaving
—CP Cavafy

When you lie awake in the early hours
with your lover still and fast asleep,
listen for the sounds beyond your window –
the wind, the storm-tossed trees, coyotes crying—and do not
curse your luck that has now
failed you, or plead with the angels
who watched over and who have now left you
on your own.

Rise from your bed, go to the window
look out on the world that's leaving now.
You have prepared a lifetime for this moment,
do not let your courage fail you at the last.

Don't fool yourself, don't pretend
this world is just a dream, or deny yourself the fruits
of your mistakes.
You are still strong and vital
yet all of life is being torn from your grasp.
Face it all with eyes wide open,
standing tall, no supplicant
down on his knees.

Say goodbye to her now breathing softly,
there is no way that she can follow,
she will have to find the strength to carry on.
Say goodbye to all that you now cherish,
this world that you have built is leaving.
Say goodbye to all you now will lose.

Mike and Claire

AveAtqueVale by Judyth Hill

*For Beloved Michael Adams, Poet, Mountain Man,
Wilderness Lover, Musician, FireGiggler Extraordinaire.....*

We say you're gone,
we have only that one way
to understand our loss.

I say, here, my friend,
in our hearts
and there,

silhouetted
against range after range
of distance

perched comfortably at the edge
of the trail
in the Chinese Mountains.

Blue behind you, Blue
before you, Blue
beneath you.

We are the ones
who are gone.
You remain,

constant
to Blue Mountains,
constantly walking, there.

poet goes on
boddhisattva silence
a familiar bardo

Jimi Bernath

Gratitude by Art Goodtimes

for Crazy Cloud

that we shared this Bardo
Bought stock
in the lyric valuables

Traded rants & reveries
around a Dolores campfire
in the Chinese Mtns

Heard each other's roar
at Windy Point
& the heartsongs of
gourditas y gourditos

Made the trek up
your Wet Mtn. hill
to whisper just
a breath above the wind

You talked steel
Went deep underground

Lived as bard
fire giggler
the wobbly hobo monk
avatar of Broken Hand Peak

Blessed wild memories
Blessed be to know thee

Raindog

MELTING SNOW by G. Murray Thomas

Worn out from travel
but warm inside a friend's house
I observe,
through a frosted window:

In the sunlight outside
following an early snowstorm
golden leaves drop the unexpected weight
snow tumbling down
branches springing up.

Mu by Stewart Warren

for Michael

You say, *I know things you don't.*
But it's not grand, rather
the kind of thing a mother
or a mountain might say,
the appointed knowing
that comes with living
closer to death, to wilderness.
Today, brother, you shine—
some road dust washed off,
the weight of information slid
from the roof, so much melted snow,
grinding of axes, birthdates
and formulas to remember, all that.
And now, you know
what you've always known.

I'm sharper, you smile,
and I catch a glimpse
of that "something" climbing
out of your body, beginning to ascend.

So we're trading poems:
cold mountain for desert rant,
eating Thai curry in Lafayette. Besides,
what do those open mic junkies know?
Of course we sound like our parents!
And this summer you'll bag fourteeners
on the other side of radiation.
The air is thinner around you.
You grin a lot
for a guy whose hospital bills have six zeros.

How, I wonder, could I ever catch up,
my own debt of this doing?
Mindfulness, you say...
Enough / Not enough.
Chemo / Not Chemo.
Buddha Nature / Not Buddha Nature.

Yesterday I pulled over for a picture,
slid into a snow bank
going up Deer Creek Road. Hell yes,
I wanted to be towed out.
I used to think I'd know
exactly what I'd say
if cancer came calling.

For Michael Adams, Poet by Deborah Kelly

When Michael Adams died,
I thought of pollen,
not ash, but pollen,
ripe, drenching the invisible air with
what light can reach and color golden.

Pollen must be dispersed
and breath must be made visible,
so they join with sunlight in that angle,
disclosing poems.

Mike's Appalachia,
his steel valleys,
red wolf and white oak, live
more visible in poems than in photos.

And all the minds Mike lead to dance
his unstoppable songs,
move their feet in time over floorboards,
unfolding, joining, singing themselves awake…

for the sight
of Mike in an angle of light,
as always, across his pages.

It's All About Stone by Linn G. Baker

It's all about stone.
Grasping, groping to summit.
Pliant flesh on warm granite.

The last hike with Michael, south of Boulder, made me wish for more, but it was too late. Sunday, on a Cuchara Pass trail, a smooth, smokey quartz pebble rolled, unaccountably, across my path. The surprise and simplicity of it reminded me of Michael's poetry. I knew that I'd gotten my wish.
—Linn G. Baker

I Lent Steel Valley by Lawrence Gladeview

to a buddy
who lives in
central
pennsylvania

a few
years back
he did some
camera work
on a
pbs show
about
old buffalo's
blue collar
industry

a month
or so later
he called
to say
how much
he enjoyed
the collection's
unguarded
laughter

its
back breaking
blood

&
above all
mike's
uncanny ability

to give ink
printed
by machine

such

beautiful

texture.

LAST WORDS FOR A SHAMAN by Phil Woods

Watch old footage from the 90s
Of Mike, vigorous & on fire,
Reciting poems full of verbal heat,
Word play & shamanic incantation.
This man was in love
With land & language.
A man inspired by place,
The "din of the tribe,"
The rhythms of work &
The soundtrack of play.
R & B heard from another car
At a stoplight, a wailing saxophone
Late at night tracing the whole
River system on its way
To New Orleans, white soul
Out of the hill country,
Down home country blues,
& stinging Chicago south-side
Like Buddy, Muddy & the Wolfe.
Mike loved it all. The curve
Of the high peaks
& a dear woman's body
Seen in Laramie.
We are shooting stars
Traveling with a finite brightness.
Mike shot high
& glowed for his "gigglers."
Long may he be read
& remembered.

october twilight by John Macker

For Michael Adams

took a walk in the
october cool twilight
crossed through the rusted barbed
wire fence to the next
pasture
                              hoof holes
punched into dried mud

our quivering yellow hackberry
like Rexroth said:
the moon has a sheen
like a glacier
its harsh empty vastness
can't camouflage the sense
of whispering loss now sunk
deep within —

must've followed that spirit-
trickster han shan up into the
spanish peaks
one last breathtaking time
a few days or so before first snow
the bite in the air makes us feel like
we'll live
to climb another
thousand feet

2 ravens' rhythmic black-winged whooshes
low overhead
fills the
                    empty space
out here
between
breaths.

Strawbale by Mossbeard (Padma Thornlyre)

We do this work to learn
how we really smell, &
not for love of money.

We do this work for stout
& steak, & pinesmoke.
We do it to sleep at night.

We do this work for the crazy
clouds & rockslides, for
Cousin Bub's guitar, for

the bamboo maiden & mud-
wenches. We do this work
for our mountain lion children,

our badgers & little owls,
that they might know the cleanness
of sweat, what tribe is theirs.

We do this work for the trapper's
daughter, her childhood's starving
sheep so mercifully frozen,

the dead mound her father
left, her dog & a dozen foxes.
We do this work for the sparks

that land on Spicer's Billy the Kid,
for the hummingbirds & Sangres,
reckless sage, salmon & banjo.

We do this work because
the blisters earned
wielding pick-ax & buzzsaw,

sifting-screen & trowel
are good. We do this work
for the mathematics of stucco

in our beards, for citrus precision,
soreness of foot & the insolent
sun reminding us

that we are flesh & flesh can
sear. We do this work for our
olding bones, that our ashes

might rest in the Wet Mountain
Hardscrabble starry-starry
wind. And we do this work

for what we've scattered already,
every drop of sake we've spilt,
every seed we've sown into woman.

(note: Strawbale *first appeared in* The Blue House, *a webzine, and then in* Eating Totem: The Mossbeard Poems *by Padma Thornlyre © 2008)*

the last lonesome stars of Colorado by John Macker

*. . . that you have stolen something valuable from God Himself,
something He will soon miss and take right back.*
—Mike Adams

colorado long walking bard
han shan shadowed you up broken hand
peak
above timberline
you discovered these mountains
at 19, there in the latest snow
high over every living thing
the perfect-bodied beauty of life
or the shambolic
troubled soul of America

instead of the civilian conservation
corps implements of glorious trail
building, you climbed
equipped with a usgs topo map, some
cold mountain poems
a clear-eyed view of san luis valley &
the eternal sweat equity
of those who worked these
trails 60 years before.

these mountains herald you now
they miss you like a brother
the bold cluttered heavens
                the tough old stars
that once lulled you to sleep

that you could see clearly
from these heights
have faded for now &
left behind
the festering silence
of loss.
I know you best through your
words, we wandered

the same
tough old sangre de cristos
enough room in our rucksacks
for nanao, ed abbey, rexroth
I shared your breath as I read
your poems full of passion
& witness
each one an old soul
a wobbly song
aching with starry light &

they will
shine for me
long after the universe follows
this deepest night across colorado
towards dawn.

Not Much Has Changed by Jared Smith

Not much has changed in this death.
A child who would have been as good a friend
perhaps or had as much compassion and passion
and love of life perhaps lives somewhere,
and it does not matter that I will never know him.

I will remember the coffees at old wood tables,
the strumming of guitar, the way notes melted into pain,
the charities we organized together for the working man
knowing that we had worked the hot steel ovens of the 60s
and each alone had headed out across the desert of America
and each alone had found our love and wives and peace
sooner than we should but too far from where we started.

These are personal things that do not mean a damn
to those things that we both believed in. The sun rising
beyond the mountains on an autumn morning. The aspen
going gold into the slow detritus of the coming winter
and the wind whipping mountain peaks even as today.
A colder time is coming warmed only by memory.
Not much has changed, and he would say the same.

EVERYTHING IS IN FRONT OF US by Judyth Hill

For Mike Adams

When I stop speaking,
this poem
will open its wings.

Take the palomino's reins,
 turn his head toward the mountains,
feast the Beloved on clover's honied translation,
marigold and amaranth.

The meadow calls to us in vine, in leaves
going so gently – away.

Look in the mirror, and be seen by infinite varieties of light.
This rose, this outcry of swallow's flight –
What wings do we wear at journey's end?

See the road, see it?
Stop in certainty there,
Praising the vivid harvest.

Prairies stretch before us in the reverie of bells,
in the play of chime and destined ring.

Toll, toll. Ache for an understanding of thorns,
the pierce of absence.

On this map, learn the latitude of angels.

Memorize the latticed patterns of coral.
Clamor for the overhead passing of the Perseid,
become egrets by morning.

Sit your heart where your mind is.
Speak from underneath
the buddleia, butterfly bush, when

those leaves fall,
watch for wings everywhere
.

Mike 3, 10-1 by Jerry Smaldone

*"sometimes you have to laugh about it
all to maintain a healthy perspective."*

I turn on the car to go to work
and the radio blasts music.
I never listen to music in the car.
Well, rarely. My wife must have
used the car last night.

It's Springsteen's "Thunder Road".
A chill runs through me, taking me
back to the last time I saw Mike,
eyes mostly open for the first time

in a month, open as his soul
as he took in all my jabber while
Bruce bellowed in the background
and his hand lay in mine.

Claire says he's angry that this has
happened, this interruption in
his treatment, this solitary chaplet,
a place of prayer along the painful
and confusing road to death.

I turn up the sound and let it soak
into my anger, reach into the corners
to wrench out the depression, the dark
gray emptiness that prevents feeling.

The song ends and I turn the radio off
lost in some oblivion of why do I feel so
bad and why have I seen so much death.
There is no answer.

I pull into work and sit numbly until
it hits me. Of course, it was Mike,
saying hello, saying carry on, saying
the road is wild and beautiful, saying

Be as strong in life as I was facing death.
and I wonder at his new journey,
at what his soul sees
and the thought helps me
for awhile. Thanks, Mike

Photo by Linn G. Baker

Practicing Tai Chi in Elks Park with Mike
by Rosemerry Wahtola Trommer

Though I did not understand
what the movements meant,
I followed him the best I could,
let my body move through the morning air
the way his body moved—
white cranes spreading our wings,
standing first on one leg and then on the other,
one hand moving further and faster than the other.
If someone had touched me, I would have collapsed,
but Mike, he was like the mountain
we were standing beside, perhaps
like a mountain with wings.
It was one of those moments
that we don't know at the time
will be a moment we always return to—
but here I am again, October morning,
cold, dawn light, the sun still crouched
behind the mountain, one of a handful
of white cranes landed in Elks Park,
waiting for the perfect moment to strike.

The Day After He Died by Rosemerry Wahtola Trommer

—for Crazy Cloud

It is raining and sometimes
it is snow. In the gutter
outside my window the stones
are gray and rose, equal parts
dingy and glittersome.
Across the way, the spruce tree
is more blue than green.
Its trunk is crooked. Its boughs
uneven. On a day such as this
it is so human to want to seek warmth,
to want to lean whatever in us
is crooked and blue toward another's
crooked blueness and find

some communion there. So human
to want to say something true,
perhaps about how fragile
this life is, perhaps about love,
but these truths are like
the simplest stones,
changing color each time
we try to describe them.
Easier to say it is raining
and sometimes it is snow.
Though already the clouds
are clearing. Already the spruce
gathers late morning sun
in fat droplets that hang
under needles. I am walking
around the things I do not wish
to say as much as those that I do.
Like he's gone. Like it hurts.
Like it's fragile, this life, though he was
strong. Like he was never ours.

Rosemerry says about Mike, "I loved his quick smile, his gentleness, his encouraging nature, his ability to move through worlds."

ON THE DEATH OF MIKE ADAMS by Raindog

His poetry could be
As brisk as the air on any
Mountain meadow or as
Sweet as a good woman's smile

He was a kind and
Generous man whom
Rumor has it never
Got mad but he was
Also the kind of man
That you knew you didn't
Want to fuck with

Even death knew this
Death had to come at
Him sideways when
He wasn't lookin'
Death can be chicken
Shit like that

But even a cheap
Shot like that
Can't diminish
What Mike
Meant

He was a real human
Being and a good one
At that and now
That he's gone
It will take at least
Five good men to
Carry-on where
He left off

Lone Wolf by Roseanna Frechette

Live in the skin
of a lone wolf
track eye of the enemy
eye of life source
source no other wolf sees.
Breathe up through thick fur
all covered with snow
pulling shadow at dawn
crossing thin ice alone
is survival
some creatures know this
sadness
gold pebbles
stream bed lays out
for stream carry away.

This poem first appeared in Mad Blood Issue #1, *in which much of Mike's work also appeared. It was written around the time I met Mike, with his passion for wolf preservation and his dedicated work with the organization* Sinapu *as well as the dedication to artistic solitude we shared.*

Elegy for Michael Adams by Padma Thornlyre
(5/18/49 - 9/26/13)
in three parts

1.
August 25, 2013
Tough Old Buzzard

When Rockslide XIV
called me at work, saying,
"You need to get down here, Buddy,"

the first bird I saw
was a great blue heron
lumbering through the sky
as though bearing
the crazy weight of clouds
upon his back, and then

I saw a red-tailed hawk,
ubiquitous in Evergreen.

How do you drive
when you're trembling like this?

We've come to call you back
from the abyss,

from the cancer and the chemo
and that mean-spirited
infection that struck you
right when you had
no white blood cells to speak of.
We've come to call you
back from the fever—
with Whitman and Welch
and your own words, too,
and what words

we can muster
in books we have written
ourselves.

We call you back with banjo
and sutra,
we call you back through
our stinging eyes
and we dance for you,
some of us singing
and some of us trying
to sing.

Those who know
how to, pray.
Know of those
who do not pray
that our love
is nevertheless
an equal love,

and if the gods already
inhabit us
or if they listen
when we speak to them,
they surely know already

what lies within us
when we have need of them,
and will come to us unbeckoned
because they want to
and because it is within
their power and their means.

2.
September 27, 2013
Bodhissatva

for The Ancient Order, upon the death of our friend Michael Adams, and borrowing a line from Rockslide XIV

We lost a Fire Giggler
last night, one of our

own, maybe the best
of us, our companion

under the sparks
of a one-match fire

below quilted stars
that weighed upon us

rawly, like pelts
against the cold,

or turkey buzzards
circling. I couldn't

find my glasses this
morning. I don't recall

where I put them
down. It will be hard

to see, today at work,
washing dishes,

washing off what's left
of today's special,

lobster mac & cheese
& keeping up

with the silverware.
We need a good scout,

Crazy Cloud, a scout
with a clawhammer

banjo. We're tailing
you, we're right behind.

I see ahead of you
a brilliant boy

laughing in a blue
cloud of butterflies.
I've heard it's best
to shun the well

of forgetfulness,
though its waters

be cold, sweet and
so very welcome

after the long slog
between this and

what's next; seek
the well-guarded

grove, instead.
Answer that you

were once a child
of both Earth

and the stars,
but are now

a child
of the stars alone.

> 3.
> *October 1, 2013*
> **Tough Old Buzzard**

> We lost you last Thursday,
> Michael, but you were
> one tough old buzzard.

Holdin' on like that?
That was badass.

You grabbed onto the crown
of a great blue spruce
and nearly leapt off
that heron's blue back.

But he was even
tougher — and now,
together, you've

flown

too
high.

Courtesy of Padma Thornlyre

Too Soon by Raindog

So much depends on the grinning of
a lone child
laughing, on the run
like Neruda's brown and agile,
at loose ends
with seaweed hair,
floating free, unadorned.

A simple grace

Too soon
the weight of anguish,
a carpet of lilies
on fields of Flanders, Belfast,
Soweto, Compton, Sarajevo, Beruit.

Too soon
the tolling of the bell
Too soon
the world is
at once,
bigger
and yet (somehow)
smaller.

Too soon
the long night,
like a blanket,
covers us all.

For All of Us by James Taylor III

The wind tears through us
undeterred like a cancer.
It's a life time blown down and swept away
from Pittsburg to Boulder,
Buffalo to dusty Badlands.
We not only carry *On the Road*
in our hip hip pockets, day packs and modern
rucksacks
but in our hearts.

We are Rogue Scholars
Sagebrush Sleuths
Mountaintop Misfits
that won't work for wages
but are willing to bust our backs
to stand together.

We have faced
the faces of God alone,
in our lovers, our children,
wives and witnesses,
and within the boundless energy of
rising rock and fire.

And that boundless energy can be contained
in memories,
vast readings
campfires
river roads
yurts, tipis, straw baled and mud humped
abodes,
or when cloistered
in a solemn room
gathered around a hospital bed.

Whenever that cancerous wind blows
wherever it tries to penetrate
and blow down what makes us human,
attempting to break apart the spirit or dry out the blood,
our brotherly bonds
stand firm.

And when angels look to the open road
they will hear the fossil fuel cowboys singing
Death Don't Have No Mercy
In This Land.

And those very same angels
in a circle of fire
will testify
to the standing power
of mountains
the eternal power of heart.

Michael Adams died on September 26, 2013, surrounded by family and friends.

Mike was born in Pittsburgh, PA on May 18, 1949 and grew up in the steel town of Homestead. Colorado had been his home for over 30 years.

Mike's life and work were a reflection of his own intellectual curiosity and varied interests. He spent four years as a steelworker at the Duquesne works while he attended the University of Pittsburgh, where he received a Bachelor's degree in anthropology, and a Master's degree in planning. He continued his education at the Jack Kerouac School of Disembodied Poetics at Naropa University in Boulder Colorado. Mike also pursued a Zen meditation practice, which informed and shaped his later artistic activities.

After his stint as a steelworker, Mike worked as an urban planner, mountaineering guide, teacher, and natural resource manager. His recent career included work for Boulder County Open Space as a natural resource manager, and as a faculty advisor for the Masters' program in Adventure Education at Prescott University.

His diverse work experience and upbringing left him with a lifelong passion for issues of social, economic, and environmental justice and a love for the natural world. Mike spent much time hiking and exploring in the mountains of Colorado. He especially loved being at the cabin he built in the Wet Mountains.

Mike was very active in poetry and the arts, both locally and regionally. He was active in, and for a time chaired, the Lafayette, Colorado Cultural Arts Commission. Mike was himself an accomplished and highly regarded poet and writer. His poems, essays, and reviews have appeared in numerous journals, magazines and anthologies, including *The Pedestal, PoLarity, The Midwest Quarterly, Pilgrim-age, Mad Blood, Hunger* and *Thirst*, and *Desert Shovel*. He was also an accomplished musician and clawhammer banjo player, and often merged his poetry with music. He was a Guest Artist with Art From Ashes, and performed on radio and television across the country, either alone or as part of the poetry group The Free Radical Railroad. Throughout his life, Mike stayed true to his roots, his principles and his beliefs, and advocated tirelessly on be-half of justice and equality, in his poetry, in his music and in his life.

Michael published seven books of poetry: *Steel Valley, If You Can Still Dance With It: Stone Belly and Cold Mountain, Whistleblowers: The Free Radical Rail-road, Broken Hand Peak, Underground: Free Radical Railroad, Blue Flowered Lettuce*, and *Hardscrabble*, and edited another, *Singing This Great Body Together: In Remembrance of September 11, 2011*. He was the winner of the 2007 Mark Fischer Poetry Prize.

Michael was deeply loved and respected by everyone who knew him for his greatness of spirit, his kindness and humility, his rectitude and intellectual honesty, and the thoughtfulness and integrity with which he approached everyone around him and everything he did. Those who knew him will always remember his wise counsel, his good cheer around the campfire, his hearty laugh, his poetry, and his banjo playing and singing. His friends regarded him as their brother, and his community of family and friends will miss him deeply.

Mike is survived by his beloved wife Claire, mother Martha, mother-in-law Margaret, sister Jeanne and her partner Lavon, brother Mark and wife Lynne, sister-in-law Colleen and husband Ray, brother-in-law Dan and his wife Li-Piin, nephews Andy and wife LeeAnn, Kaleb and wife Loretta and great-nephew Jakob, niece Heather and husband Simon and great nephew Dylan, faithful canine companion Terra, a large extended family and his many, many friends (some of whom have contributed to this chapbook).

Donations in Mike's honor can be made to the Leukemia and Lymphoma Society, Rocky Mountain Chapter, www.lls.org, or Community FoodShare at *www.communityfoodshare.org*

Jim Bernath

This book was conceived, solicited, assembled and printed by RD Armstrong of LUMMOX Press in loving memory of his friend, Mike Adams, who passed away too soon (or so it seems to us, the ones who must walk this earth without him).

The layout was done by Chris Yeseta.

The LUMMOX Press publishes chapbooks like this one, the Little Red Book series, a series of Trade paperback books (the Respect series), the LUMMOX poetry anthology (yearly) and e-books.

The stated goal of the press is to elevate the bar for poetry, while bringing the 'word' to an international audience. We are proud to offer this chapbook as part of that effort.

For more information and to see our growing catalog of titles, please go to *www.lummoxpress.com/lc*

www.ingramcontent.com/pod-product-compliance
Lightning Source LLC
Chambersburg PA
CBHW070041070426
42449CB00012BA/3127